A Tribute to
THE YOUNG AT HEART

Judith Viorst

By Jill C. Wheeler

Published by Abdo & Daughters, 4940 Viking Drive, Suite 622, Edina, Minnesota 55435.

Copyright © 1997 by Abdo Consulting Group, Inc., Pentagon Tower, P.O. Box 36036, Minneapolis, Minnesota 55435 USA. International copyrights reserved in all countries. No part of this book may be reproduced in any form without written permission from the publisher.

Printed in the United States.

Cover and Interior Photo credits: Wide World Photos
                                    Atheneum Books for Young Readers--Didi Cutler

Edited by Lori Kinstad Pupeza

Library of Congress Cataloging-in-Publication Data

Wheeler, Jill C., 1964-
    Judith Viorst / Jill C. Wheeler.
    p.   cm. -- (A tribute to the young at heart)
    Includes Index.
    Summary: A biography of the writer whose work includes children's picture books, poetry, and non-fiction for adults.

    ISBN 1-56239-788-5

    1. Viorst, Judith--Biography--Juvenile literature. 2. Women authors, American --20th century--Biography--Juvenile literature. 3. Children's literature-- Authorship--Juvenile literature. [1. Viorst, Judith. 2. Authors, American. 3. Women--Biography.]
    I. Title. II. Series.
    PS3572.I6Z96   1997
    818' .5409--dc21
    [B]   97-10224
                                                                 CIP
                                                                  AC

Table of Contents

MAKING THE BEST OF A VERY BAD DAY

Young Alexander Viorst was having a bad day. Nothing was going right. His mother, poet and author Judith Viorst, thought about how she handled bad days. She realized it was important to accept that it was a bad day and go on.

"I observed that the concept of 'I'm having a bad day,' seemed to help adults get through those bad days a little better," she said. "And so I wrote about such a day for Alexander, who was having a lot of them."

The result was *Alexander and the Terrible, Horrible, No Good, Very Bad Day*. In the book, Alexander wakes up with gum in his hair. His mother forgets to put his dessert in his lunch bag. He has a cavity. He gets scolded for fighting. He has to suffer through lima beans at supper and kissing on TV that night. By the end of the day, Alexander is ready to move to Australia. Yet his mother reminds him that some days are just like that, even in Australia.

Alexander and the Terrible, Horrible, No Good, Very Bad Day has made a lot of kids —and their parents—feel better. It has become one of Viorst's most popular books. Like many of her other books, it is a funny look at the events that happen in her own family.

"Most of my children's books are for or about my own children," she said. "Mostly, they're written to meet certain needs. For instance, when Anthony was mercilessly persecuting his younger brother I decided to write *I'll Fix Anthony* to cheer up Nick."

Viorst's work also has cheered up adults. She has written five books of poems for adults, as well as five non-fiction books. Many readers of *Redbook* magazine have enjoyed her work over the years as a contributing editor. She also has written poems and articles for *The New York Times*,

Holiday , *Washingtonian,* and *Writer* magazines.
Publishers have translated some of her children's stories
into Dutch, French, German, Japanese, and Spanish.

Judith Viorst.

ROSES ARE RED, THE DOG IS DEAD

Judith Viorst (pronounced "*vee*-orst") was born Judith Stahl on February 2, 1931 in Newark, New Jersey. Her father, Martin Leonard Stahl, was an accountant. Her mother was named Ruth June Stahl.

Judith says she has always been writing, "or at least since I was seven or eight when I composed an ode to my dead parents, both of whom were alive and well and, when they read my poem, extremely annoyed," she said.

"I always, always, always wanted to be a writer," she said. "I never wanted to be anything else—never. It never entered my mind that I was going to earn a living at it or be well-known as a result of it."

Judith carefully printed up her first poems and sent them off to magazines. They quickly came back to her. "They were terrible poems—about dead dogs, mostly," she recalled. She kept writing in spite of the rejections and received even more rejections. She said that part of the reason for these rejections might be that she wrote about serious things such as ". . . the meaning of life. Death. Pain. Suicide. That sort of thing."

After graduating from high school, Judith attended Rutgers University in New Brunswick, New Jersey. Her scholarship earned her a place in the Phi Beta Kappa organization. Phi Beta Kappa is an American honorary academic society. Only outstanding scholars can be members. Judith graduated with a bachelor of arts degree from Rutgers with honors.

Through it all, she wrote. As she recalls, she worked steadily but remained unpublished. "I worked for a confessions magazine, I wrote a confessions story. I worked for a fashion magazine, I wrote a fashion story. I worked in a children's book publishing house, I wrote a children's book. Everything got turned down. I was also sending out science fiction stories and poems. I was a very busy little bee, but I was a total flop."

Judith's luck at getting published began to change after she met and married another writer. His name was Milton Viorst. The two of them settled in Washington, D.C., where Milton was a political reporter and writer. Soon after, the *New York Herald Tribune* hired Judith as a stringer.

The *Herald Tribune* hired Judith to report on parties in Washington, D.C. Unfortunately, she found she needed help. "I could never recognize anyone famous," she remembered. "Milton had to go everywhere with me." Judith used her tie with the newspaper to begin writing more than stories about parties. She began writing poems for the paper's Sunday magazine section.

A SCIENTIFIC START

Most young readers know Judith for her fictional picture books. Yet her early work was in non-fiction.

Judith's first venture in book publishing came in 1961. She and another woman edited the book *Wonderful World of Science*. The following year, Judith wrote *Projects: Space*. She followed that with *One Hundred and Fifty Science Experiments, Step-by-Step* published in 1963. In 1965, she published a book about animals.

In 1967, Judith tackled the subject of earth sciences. She wrote a book about the many aspects of geology. The book talks about everything from rocks and minerals to glaciers, earthquakes, and volcanoes.

Judith stopped writing about science after that. She wanted to focus on her poetry instead. Earlier, she had put the poems that were published in the *New York*

Herald Tribune into a book. *The Village Square* became her first poetry book. It wouldn't be the last.

A book by Judith Viorst.

POEMS ON THE LIGHTER SIDE

Judith's next book of poems came out in 1968. *It's Hard to Be Hip over Thirty and Other Tragedies of Married Life* became an instant bestseller. Millions of people enjoyed Judith's funny, light-hearted verses. However, Judith says it's just as hard to write light verse as it was to write the more serious poems of her youth.

"I slave over them," she said of her poems. "It always makes me feel embarrassed to say how hard I work on them because they are 'light verse,' and yet it took me four years to write the 24 poems in *How Did I Get to Be Forty and Other Atrocities*."

Judith's success comes from her sharp insights into daily life. She credits that ability to her husband and three sons, Anthony, Nick, and Alexander. "Someone once remarked to me that if I hadn't gotten married, I might have written the great American novel. But I think if I hadn't gotten married, maybe I wouldn't have written anything."

"Milton and my life with him have given me the encouragement I needed to pursue writing. . . ," she said. "I don't think it's a coincidence that I never had anything published before I was married to Milton."

"Married life is the rock on which I sit and do my work," she said. "The kids' role in this should not be dismissed. It is possible to find delight in just hanging around the kitchen while one kid is making a chicken sandwich and the other is tossing a napkin into the trash and missing."

WRITE ME A STORY, MOMMY

Judith's children frequently inspire her writing. "Four of the books that I've written for children I consciously sat down and wrote because one child or another of mine had a problem," she said in an interview in 1976. " . . . and while I was surely not foolish enough to expect that any book I wrote would solve these problems, I hoped it might help my boys to laugh at their problems, or look at them in less troubled, less hopeless ways."

That was the case with her book *The Tenth Good Thing about Barney*. The book is about a boy whose cat named Barney has died. The boy's mother asks him to think of ten good things to say about Barney at the cat's funeral. The boy can only think of nine. Later, the boy discovers the tenth thing: burying Barney will help the flowers and grass grow. *Barney* was published in 1971. It also won the Silver Pencil Award.

"When a lot of questions about death were being raised around our house, my struggle for a way to respond to those questions resulted in the Barney book," she said. Two years later, she published *My Mommy Says There Aren't Any Zombies, Ghosts, Vampires, Creatures, Demons, Monsters, Fiends, Goblins, or Things* for her son Nick.

Likewise, *Sunday Morning* is about a mother and father who are out late Saturday night. They ask their two boys not to wake them early the next morning. "We do not want to hear anything until 9:45 a.m.," the father tells them. "And we'll tell you when that is." However, the younger boy awakes at 5 a.m. He then wakes up his brother. The two mess up one room after another in their house, while their parents try to sleep.

Between writing books, Judith wrote a syndicated column for the *Washington Star Syndicate* in 1970-1972. She also wrote many articles for *Redbook* magazine. Several of those articles earned her awards too.

KID POEMS

By this time, Judith had written several books of poetry for adults. Now she began a poetry book for children. *If I Were in Charge of the World and Other Worries* is a collection of poems for children and their parents. The poems deal with many common issues of young people. There's a poem about having a girlfriend who's taller than oneself. Another poem talks about the need for healthier hamsters and lower basketball hoops.

Another poem is a remake of the Cinderella story. In this version, Cinderella decides she doesn't like the prince after all. She pretends the glass slipper doesn't fit her!

BACK TO SCHOOL

Judith's life took a different turn in 1980. Her youngest son, Alexander, had just gone off to college. Judith decided to go back to school, too. She enrolled at the Washington Psychoanalytic Institute. She wanted to study clinical psychology.

"What was in my mind was my wish at that particular time in my life to deepen and enlarge upon my resources for writing about what I always write about . . . people's inner emotional lives and their relationships with each other," she said. "I'm interested in people's fears and dreams and hopes and love lives and jealousies and pleasures and motivations . . . .

"Going back to school was really one of the great thrilling experiences of my life," she said. "I had originally thought that I would just take everything I was learning and keep doing the same kind of writing . . . . Psychoanalytic theory made me realize that everything I heard and saw could be better understood with it. And then I knew that I wanted to write more directly about it."

Judith used what she learned in school to write a new book for adults. As it sounds, *Necessary Losses* is all about loss. It features Judith's poetry, along with psychoanalytic theory, interviews, and her personal experiences. It talks about the different ways that people deal with loss. It also shows how no one can avoid loss.

Judith Viorst relaxing at home.

THE GOOD-BYE BLUES

Judith returned to working on children's picture books in 1988. This time she wrote *The Good-bye Book*. In this book, a little boy does everything he can to stop his parents from going out for the evening.

"It's probably one of the most common experiences that occurs between a child and his parents," Judith said. "That tussle when you're going out and your child doesn't want you to leave."

The little boy in *The Good-bye Book* tries guilt. He tries persuasion. He fakes being sick. He gets angry. Nothing works. Finally, he's alone with the baby-sitter. In the end, he finds his evening much more enjoyable than he thought it would be.

The boy in *The Good-bye Book* is like many of Judith's child characters—he's not perfect. She likes it that way. "Kids need to encounter kids like themselves," she said. "Kids who can sometimes be crabby and fresh and rebellious, kids who talk back and disobey, tell fibs and get into trouble, and are nonetheless still likable and redeemable."

Judith said it surprised her when she wrote *The Good-bye Book* to discover that no one had tackled that topic before. Fortunately for parents, she did. Now parents can use the book to talk and learn about separation.

WORKING MOM

Throughout her career, Judith has enjoyed combining writing with being a wife and mother. Her work has given her the flexibility to do volunteer work and spend plenty of time with her family.

"It's quite terrific to be a working mother whose research, for the most part, consists of hanging around the house. Since my husband also works at home (and can make lunch) it's altogether a very pleasant arrangement. He is the harshest critic and greeter and encourager of my books, and without him there wouldn't be any."

Judith says she and Milton frequently help each other with their writing. "We read each other's work, help each other think of synonyms when we can't think of a word, and all the rest of it," she said.

"Of course, we have the great advantage of writing about very different areas," she added. "I don't know how wonderful it would be if we were in a competitive situation, both writing children's books or both writing on politics. My husband is a political specialist, probably one of the country's leading experts on the Middle East, and not madly informed about poetry, as I am not madly informed about the Middle East. So it works out very well."

Fortunately, Judith has the discipline required to work at home. "I pretty much get up in the morning and write," she said. "I organize my life very efficiently. . . . I never talk on the phone without keeping my hands busy.

"I have a certain quota for myself in the writing. . . . my general quota is a poem a month. I write a *Redbook* column nine times a year, and that's on a fixed schedule. I'm very disciplined by nature, so it isn't a big psychological achievement for me to get my work done in an orderly fashion. It would be a big psychological achievement for me to hang loose."

Even though Judith's children are grown, she stays in touch with what it's like to be young. "I have friends of all different ages, including friends with little kids and friends who are grandparents of little kids. And people tell me stories about their kids because they know I'm interested. I have a very good memory for everybody's kid stories."

Judith enjoys working at home.

A DREAM
COME TRUE

Judith always is willing to try new things. She wrote a
musical called *Happy Birthday and Other Humiliations*.
She also wrote a series of poetic monologues for CBS
television called "Annie: The Women in the Life of a Man."
Her work on "Annie" earned her an Emmy Award in 1970.

Despite the breadth of her work, she says children's
books have a special place in her heart. "At their best,
their language, their art, their seriousness of intent
measure up to any standards of excellence," she said.
"And the beauties and truths and delights that they can
offer to our children can meet the deepest needs of the
heart and the mind."

"It's a dream come true, exactly what I've always wanted
to do," she said of her writing career. "I have the freedom,
the independence, the flexibility—following no one's

schedule but my own, being able to tailor my schedule to the needs of my household and three children . . . .

"My experiences have exceeded my expectations, and I do think these are the best years of my life," she added. "I know what I love. I have what I love and I love what I have."

Judith won an Emmy Award in 1970.

WRITINGS

Judith Viorst has tickled many funny bones with her stories and poems. Try one of her books when you need a good chuckle.

Projects: Space, Washington Square Press, 1962

One Hundred and Fifty Science Experiments, Step-by-Step, Bantam, 1963

Natural World, Bantam, 1965

The Changing Earth, Bantam, 1967

Sunday Morning, Harper, 1968

I'll Fix Anthony, Harper, 1969

Try It Again, Sam: Safety When You Walk, Lothrop, 1970

The Tenth Good Thing about Barney, Atheneum, 1971

Alexander and the Terrible, Horrible, No Good, Very Bad Day, Atheneum, 1972

My Mama Says There Aren't Any Zombies, Ghost, Vampires, Creatures, Demons, Monsters, Fiends, Goblins, or Things, Atheneum, 1973

Rosie and Michael, Atheneum, 1974

Alexander, Who used to Be Rich Last Sunday, Atheneum, 1978

The Good-bye Book, Atheneum, 1988

The Alphabet from Z to A: With Much Confusion on the Way, Atheneum, 1994

Alexander, who's not (Do you hear me? I mean it!) Going to move, Atheneum, 1995

Sad Underwear and Other Complications: More Poems for Children and Their Parents, Atheneum, 1996

GLOSSARY OF TERMS

Atrocities — Very bad acts.

Contributing editor — A person who writes for a publication regularly.

Geology — The branch of science that deals with the history of the Earth.

Glacier — A large body of slow-moving ice.

Honors—(To graduate with honors) to earn high grades in school.

Monologue — A long speech.

Persecute — To cause someone to suffer.

Psychology — The branch of science that deals with the mind and behavior.

Stringer — A person who writes for a publication that is in another place.

Suicide — When someone takes his or her own life.

Synonyms — Different words that have the same meaning.

Index